TOILET HUMOUR

A selection of bad taste cartoons from the Silvey–Jex Partnership

D1810434

© SILVEY-JEX PARTNERSHIP 1980.
FIRST PRINTED IN ENGLAND BY MERLIN COLOUR PRINTERS, CANVEY ISLAND.
ISBN 0907280013

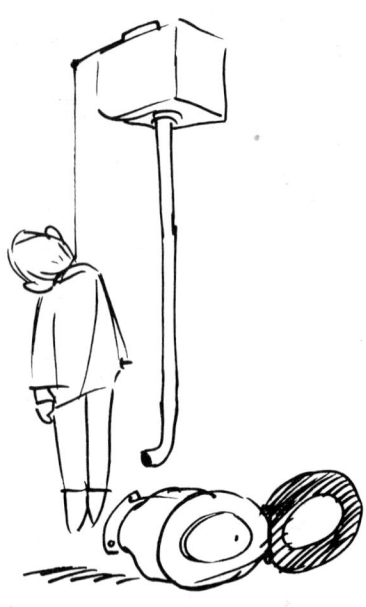

"Come on Parker – we know you're in there."

"Excuse me, but are there two 'p's in nipple?"

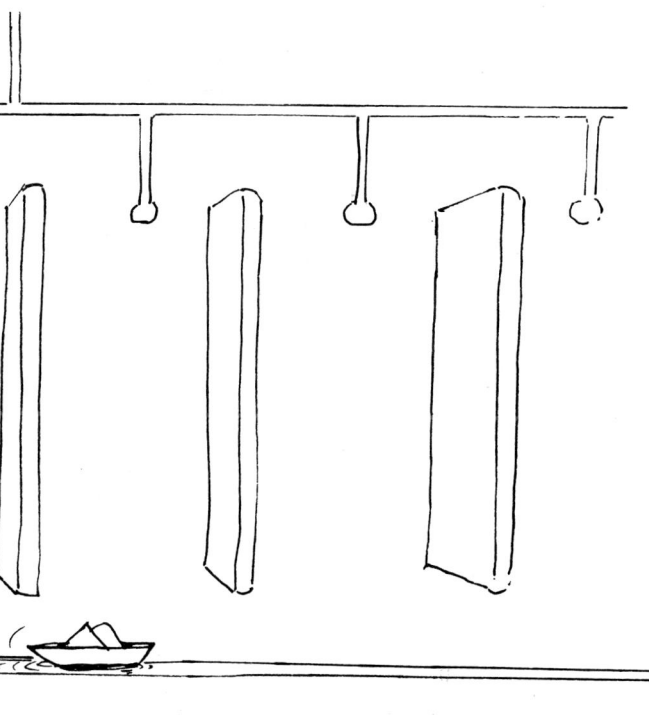

"Ouch"!

"I think you should have tried the little fellow on the potty first."

*"For God's sake Richard stop making a fuss
or the Robinsons will think you didn't enjoy the meal."*

"...and out the back here is a little chemical toilet."

"You rang my Lord"?